winning
softball

winning softball

**JOAN JOYCE and JOHN ANQUILLARE
with Dave Klein**

Henry Regnery Company•Chicago

Library of Congress Cataloging in Publication Data

Joyce, Joan.
  Winning softball.

  Includes index.
  1. Softball.   I. Anquillare, John, joint author.
II. Klein, Dave, joint author.   III. Title.
GV881.J69   796.357'8   75-1019
ISBN 0-8092-8430-8
ISBN 0-8092-8429-4 pbk.

Published by Henry Regnery Company
            180 North Michigan Avenue
            Chicago, Illinois 60601
Manufactured in the United States of America
Library of Congress Catalog Card Number: 75-1019
International Standard Book Number: 0-8092-8430-8 (cloth)
                                    0-8092-8429-4 (paper)
Published simultaneously in Canada by
Fitzhenry & Whiteside Limited
150 Lesmill Road
Don Mills, Ontario M3B 2T5
Canada

Photography by Dwight Johnson except for photos on pages
2, 4, 8, 9, 54, 66, 70

contents

preface

Softball, which was for many years a recreational sport of the United States exclusively, now has a home in almost every country in the world.

The game originated in the United States in the late 1800s and quickly became a popular pastime at picnics, playgrounds, and in backyards. It was almost 35 years, however, before enough people decided it was time to get the sport organized. At first, individual promoters and local independent groups wanted no part of organization; they feared it would deprive them of a "fast buck" or of their individual identity. So dozens of different playing rules and rules of eligibility were used all over the country.

But, in 1933, the Amateur Softball Association (ASA) and the International Joint Rules Committee on Softball were organized. These two groups, which are the governing groups for softball today, standardized rules and organized national championships. Championships were included for women, as well as for men, which has insured the importance of women's role in softball's development and growth. The list of great teams and players on the feminine side of the ledger equals and at times surpasses that of men.

Though World War II took some steam out of softball domestically, it was a major vehicle in the sport's introduction overseas. Thousands of GIs played softball all over the world—on Pacific atolls, in Asian jungles, on the lowlands of Europe.

After the war, domestic interest revived, too, and hundreds of thousands of teams sprang up to play in any vacant lot large enough to accommodate a softball diamond. The size of the diamond was, in fact, a positive point for the sport. Because it was half the size of a baseball diamond, a playing field could be located practically in any small area.

Industry became a big supporter and sponsor of softball; industrial play became so popular that, in 1957, the ASA established a separate division of championship play strictly for industrial teams. Today, national championship teams are sponsored by some of the best known companies in America, including Dow Chemical, Kodak, Briggs Manufacturing, Raybestos-Manhattan, Jax Brewery and Zollner Pistons. In addition to those that have nailed down national championships, many other well-known companies continue to support and send squads to national competitions each year—IBM, Sears, Wilson, AMF, Westinghouse, J.C. Penney, Western Electric, Aetna Insurance, Xerox, Avco-Lycoming, the airlines, and many others.

And on the international scene, softball is now played on a major competitive level in some 50 countries. International championships are held on a regular basis with as many as 20 countries competing for the coveted World Championship title.

In the meantime, another kind of softball is becoming popular in the United States. During the forties and fifties, softball was mainly a fast-pitch game. But, today, slow-pitch softball is also becoming quite popular. Slow-pitch softball, in which the pitch is required to be thrown so that it can be hit, began to be played more frequently in the early sixties and has made steady progress ever since.

The phenomenal growth of slow-pitch softball sometimes results in serious problems concerning adequate playing facilities. Recreation and park departments are frequently inundated with teams who want to play but do not have a diamond.

However, fast-pitch softball continues to be the most popular game internationally. Slow-pitch softball has not caught on outside the United States. But if growth in this country is indicative of the future, this form of softball is sure to spread to foreign lands.

Many people ask why softball is so popular. Why do over 26 million adults and youngsters play the sport on a competitive basis in the United States and another 5 million worldwide? The answer is that competition can be geared to participation on almost any level. No one is left out. It's the "game everyone can play!"

Don Porter
Executive Director
American Softball Association

introduction

Since softball is a universally popular pastime, it is important to have as many different points of view as possible represented in a book about this sport. Joan Joyce and John Anquillare play different positions on different teams and began to play for different reasons.

JOAN JOYCE

In 1962, the Waterbury, Connecticut, Police Department sponsored a charity softball game. The Raybestos Brakettes, several times national champions, were invited to play. As an added attraction,

Baseball Hall of Fame member Ted Williams, said to be the finest hitter in the history of the major leagues, was invited to hit against the Brakettes' pitcher.

Her name was Joan Joyce.

"After it was finished, I really felt bad," Joan recalls today. "I should have let him hit some."

Let him hit some? Ted Williams? The man who, while a member of the Boston Red Sox, won the American League batting championship six times, and is still the last man in the major leagues to bat over .400? What happened?

"Well, he came up for a while, maybe 10 minutes. In that time, I threw between 30 and 40 pitches. He fouled one off. I think he might have hit one. And that was it. I was throwing in a competitive sense, meaning I was trying to get him out. And I must assume he was hitting competitively, especially after the first five minutes or so. But he just couldn't touch my pitches. He was very upset, and finally threw the bat down and walked away."

A crowd of 18,000 watched. And cheered.

Accomplishments

Joan Joyce is 33 years old, and she is to women's softball what Babe Ruth was to baseball, what O. J. Simpson is to football, what Secretariat was to Thoroughbred racing. She has been called "one of the three best pitchers in softball," and the other two are men.

Her accomplishments read like a script for Rod Serling's "Twilight Zone." Take her performance in the 1973 Women's National Championship, for example. In a week-long, double-elimination tournament in which 18 teams played 35 games, Joan pitched all 9 of her team's games. She pitched 8 shutouts (no score by opposite team) and lost once, 1-0, on an error. She pitched 2 no-hitters (one going 11 innings, in which she recorded 22 strike-outs), 3 one-hitters, and 4 two-hitters. At one point, she racked up 23 1/3 innings of hitless pitching. She walked 1 batter and struck out 134 in batches of 22, 20, 16, 15, 14, 13, 12 (twice) and 10—in 69 2/3 innings of play.

She has won well over 400 games for the Brakettes, dating back to 1953 when she played as a 12-year-old, and lost under 30. She has pitched more than 70 no-hitters, more than 20 perfect games, and more than 250 games in which three or fewer hits were surrendered. In August of 1974, she led the Brakettes, representing the United States, to the championship of the Women's World Tournament.

Background

"When I started to pitch," she says, "I was terrible. I didn't like it, so I tried to hide from the team the fact that I did do a little pitching."

It was a workman, affixing opening-day banners to telephone poles at the Raybestos Memorial Field in Stratford (Conn.) who started her down the road to successful pitching. "I guess it was 1959 or 1960," Joan says. "I was warming up one afternoon and having all my usual troubles. I was wild, hitting batters, throwing the ball over the catcher's head.

"He climbed down from his ladder and asked me why I was using the windmill style of delivery. I told him it was the only one I knew, so he suggested I try the slingshot. I didn't know what it was, and he had to show me. I tried it, and it felt comfortable, and the guy said it shouldn't feel that comfortable, normally, so if it did I should stay with it. Almost overnight, I was pitching the ball with accuracy and speed, and when the Raybestos people saw the change, they began to tutor me.

"How? They got Johnny Spring (perhaps the finest pitcher in the game's history, now in the Softball Hall of Fame) from the men's team to work with me. He showed me the rise-ball and the drop-ball and how to throw the change-of-pace, and when I saw the ball actually rising, or dropping, it bolstered my confidence. I had never dreamed of this kind of success, but once I went to the slingshot delivery, I felt I had a chance to be pretty good."

Softball was a part of Joan's life from childhood. "My dad was a good player. He played a lot, and he was on a very high level, just a cut below the Cardinals (Raybestos' men's team). It was a major league level of softball. Well, he played almost every night, and my mother worked at night, so my brother and I had to go with him. We had no choice; either we grew up loving the game or being bored to tears, and we both loved it."

Joan is equally adept at other sports. She was a superior basketball player, earning Amateur Athletic Union (AAU) All-American honors in 1961 and in 1965. (She's 5 feet 9 inches tall and weighs 135 pounds.) And her first love isn't softball; it's golf. "There's far too great an element of luck in team sports," she says. "In golf, whatever I do is up to me. If I play well, it's because I made few mistakes. But I can pitch well and lose the game because of someone else's mistake. Right now I'm not as good a golfer as I am a basketball player or a softball player, but if I had the time to devote to golf, I truly believe I could earn the same kind of success." And probably she could.

JOHN ANQUILLARE

John Anquillare, 31, is the Raybestos Cardinals' link between baseball and softball. Called "Johnny Ankles" from high school on, John was one of those super athletes as a prepper. "Every major-league tryout I attended I was put at second base, even though my position in high school was third base. It was because of my speed. I ran the 100-yard dash in 9.8 seconds," he says, "and I weigh about 180 pounds."

He was offered 14 major-league baseball contracts, as well as more than 20 college football scholarships. "That was in 1960," he remembers, "before major league baseball put in its free-agent draft. So a lot of teams were after me. The highest offer I got was from the Dodgers, and it was for a bonus of about $20,000. But I decided to go to college first, rather than sign a contract. I went to New Haven College, which has since turned out several major leaguers. How do I look at it now? To be truthful, I think I made a mistake not taking a contract out of high school.

"There is no doubt in my mind I could hit major-league pitching consistently, but by the time I got out of college my value was almost nil. I had been hurt a few times, and trying to go to college and earn money, too, was a burden. I couldn't play as often as I had to, and I just didn't play as well, because I wasn't doing it every day."

Having decided that an opportunity in major league baseball had passed him by, John tried out for the Raybestos Cardinals, historically one of the best softball teams in the nation. His first season with the Cardinals was in 1966. He proved his worth that year by batting .282, but the best was yet to come. The next year his average rose to .298, and since then he has established hitting records that still stand. Three times he has hit over .400, that magical figure few ever reach. He hit .432 in 1968, when the Cardinals became national champions, and followed that with averages of .344, .363, .426 and .412.

COMPARISON OF MEN'S AND WOMEN'S SOFTBALL

As to whether women could play softball with and against men, John feels that, at least in softball, there is still a decided gulf between the sexes. "I admire the woman athlete," he says, "and Joan, in particular, is simply a great pitcher. But as far as women competing with men on our level of softball, I don't think any but two or three of their superstars would have a chance of being even decent players. The majority of them wouldn't even make a ball club, even as substitutes. The reactions aren't there; the speed isn't there. The fastest woman player can't compete with even an average man runner.

"In 1972, we decided a great, money-making idea would be for the Cardinals and the Brakettes to play a game. The fans in Stratford felt the Brakettes, especially with Joan pitching, would be able to beat us. So we went to the manager of their team and asked him about it. He said there was absolutely no chance, because his girls

John and Joan go over a play together.

would get hurt. He said he had seen one such game a few years earlier and they had had to call it off after four or five batters had hit,
because the ball was coming back too hard—dangerously hard."
Joan concedes the men at the highest level of softball are probably
better athletes. "They're bigger and faster," she says, "but I don't
think I'd have too much of a problem being a winning pitcher in the
major men's leagues."

John doesn't agree. "Joan is clearly the best of the women pitchers,
without a doubt, but it wouldn't be that way at all if she had to play
against the men. She wouldn't even be a good pitcher against men.
Hitting against Joan would be a break for me, a cinch. Even if she
was throwing at her distance, we'd all hit her."

But Joan has been successful pitching against men. "When I have faced them, I've pitched from the women's mound, which is only 40 feet from home plate. The men must pitch from 46 feet away. So that's one advantage I had, and if I pitched against the men for any appreciable time, they'd hit me, at least more than the women do. Because I throw pitches other women can't, or don't, they don't hit me as well, but most of the top men pitchers do throw my kind of pitches, so the men hitters are more accustomed to seeing them. But given a period of time to adjust, I think I could hold my own against their competition regularly."

Regardless of whether men and women ever play together, this game offers a great deal to all the athletes—male and female—who play it.

chapter one

history of softball

Two men are given credit for inventing the game today called softball (known in its formative years as mush ball, kitten ball and indoor baseball). It is probable that George Hancock, of the Farragut Boat Club of Chicago, Illinois, and Lewis Rober, a Minneapolis, Minnesota, fireman, began thinking of an indoor baseball-like game at approximately the same time—1887 and 1895, respectively. Since they were in different areas, each received local credit as the inventor.

Whatever the case, perhaps no game besides baseball has shown such rapid, all-inclusive growth in popularity in the last 50 years. Softball is played all over the world, on all levels of excellence from church leagues, men's clubs, women's groups and children's leagues to major softball tournaments.

Until the depression, softball was played with a bewildering number of rules and regulations. More than a dozen sizes of ball were used, for example, with at least that number of different-sized bats and playing fields. But in the 1930s softball became suddenly popular; it was a relatively inexpensive form of recreation that could be played in almost any open area—playgrounds, vacant lots, unused baseball diamonds. And, in 1933, the Amateur Softball Association (ASA) convened an inaugural meeting of what has come to be known as the International Joint Rules Committee (IJRC) on Softball. That meeting started a trend that has resulted, today, in softball regulations being unified on a worldwide level, with the official rules printed in more than a dozen languages so that the game is similar in many countries.

1

1968 World Championship softball team from the United States. The championship games were held in Oklahoma City (Courtesy ASA)

A GAME FOR EVERYONE

It is probably accurate to say that everybody has, at one time or another, played softball. And, for millions, a softball team and a softball league are as important as a bowling team or bridge club. A survey conducted in 1956 showed there were 65,210 teams registered with the ASA, playing in 8,153 leagues, 13,200 closed parks, 3,620 lighted parks and 16,203 open fields. Today, more than 25 million male and female participants play on softball diamonds in more than 50 countries on five continents.

Softball has also become a method of expression for large and small businesses, which see wisdom—and intrinsic advertising benefit—in sponsoring teams. The first national tournament of the Industrial League was held in Chicago in 1933 and was won by the J.J. Gillis Company team, a local entrant. By 1965, this original kernel of interest had taken on worldwide proportions when the first worldwide tournament was held for women in Melbourne, Australia. (The host nation registered a stunning upset in the final match by defeating the heavily favored United States team, 1-0.) In 1966, men got into the worldwide act in Mexico City; this time, the United States emerged as world champion by winning all 10 tournament games. The men successfully defended their title in the United States in 1968. In 1970, the U.S. Women's Championship team had another turn in Japan but lost in the final match—before a crowd of 30,000.

In addition to worldwide championship matches, the international flavor of the game has resulted in its inclusion on the programs of the Asian, Pan-American and Central American-Caribbean Games, as well as on later agendas of the Bolivariano and South Pacific Games.

THE AMATEUR SOFTBALL ASSOCIATION (ASA)

In the United States the ASA—affiliated with the Amateur Athletic Union (AAU), the National Recreation and Parks Association, the United States Olympic Committee, the International Softball Federation (ISF) and the National Industrial Recreation Association—is the governing body of amateur softball.

ASA's national headquarters are located in Oklahoma (2801 N.E. 50th Street, Oklahoma City 73111), which is also the site of the ASA Hall of Fame. The ASA Hall of Fame was established in 1957, at which time the first members—Sam Elliott of Atlanta, Georgia, and Harold Gears of Rochester, New York—were inducted. Open both to men and women, the 1974 total of softball Hall of Fame members was 48, which included founders, executives, and umpires, as well as players.

Member teams in the ASA play for the opportunity to compete in one of 12 national tournament championships, held annually to accommodate players of different ages, sexes, and types of softball. Though much of the softball played today in the United States is

The Amateur Softball Association's headquarters in Oklahoma City, Oklahoma. The Softball Hall of Fame is also housed here.

regulation (fast-pitch) softball, two other important forms of the game exist. In slow-pitch softball, discussed more completely in a later chapter, the ball is intentionally pitched to be hit (a pitcher is penalized if his pitches cannot be hit); this encourages more activity in the field. In another variation on regulation softball, a larger ball is used.

Therefore, national championship tournaments are held for Women's Fast-pitch, Women's Slow-pitch, Junior Girls' Fast-pitch and Junior Girls' Slow-pitch, Men's Fast-pitch, Industrial Slow-pitch (similar to men's slow-pitch), Junior Boys' Fast-pitch and Junior Boys' Slow-pitch. The ASA sponsors a few other championship tournaments for teams from secondary leagues: Open Slow-pitch, Class "A" Men's Slow-pitch, Class "A" Women's

Slow-pitch. There is also a national tournament for 16-inch softball.

As mentioned earlier, the ASA belongs to the International Softball Federation (ISF), an organization of softball organizations from 43 countries, ranging from Argentina to Venezuela, from Costa Rica to Panama, from Pakistan to Guam, from Japan to Czechoslovakia. And the board of officers includes representatives from the United States, Canada, Taiwan, South Africa, Netherlands, Antilles, Mexico, New Zealand and Holland.

But as large as the ASA and the ISF have grown and as impressive as their activity is, these organizations are only two among many. There are senior citizen's leagues, father-son leagues, mother-daughter leagues, Boy Scout and Girl Scout leagues, Sunday afternoon pickup leagues, and leagues sponsored by recreation departments. They are not organized for competition's sake but to give people who love the game an opportunity to play. And they seldom want for members.

chapter two

Equipment for a regulation softball game consists of bat, ball, glove, and field. Serious players have some uniform rules to follow as well.

BAT

According to ASA rules, the official bat must be round, and made of one piece of hardwood or from a block of wood consisting of two or more pieces of wood bonded together with an adhesive so that the grain direction of all pieces is essentially parallel to the length of the bat. Plastic and bamboo, also, are acceptable materials for construction of bats. Any laminated bat will contain only wood or adhesive, except for a clear finish.

equipment

The bat must be no more than 34 inches long and no more than 2 1/4 inches in diameter at its largest part. A tolerance of 1/32 inch is permitted to allow for expansion. The bat must have a safety grip of cork, tape or composition material, which shall not be less than 10 inches long or extend more than 15 inches from the small end of the bat. The bat shall be marked "OFFICIAL SOFTBALL" by the manufacturer.

The bat may also be made of metal. The bat shall have no exposed rivets, pins, rough or sharp edges, or any form of exterior fastener that would present a hazard. All exposed surfaces of the bat shall be smooth and free of burrs. A metal bat shall not have a wooden handle. It shall conform to all of the above specifications with the exception that it is metal.

Regulation softball bat. (Courtesy Dudley Sports Company, Dublin, Pennsylvania)

8

Regulation (12-inch) softball. (Courtesy Dudley Sports Company, Dublin, Pennsylvania)

BALL

The official softball is a regular, smooth-seam, concealed-stitch, or flat-surfaced ball, not less than 11 7/8 inches nor more than 12 1/8 inches in circumference. It must weigh no less than 6 1/4 ounces but no more than 7 ounces.

The center of the ball may be made either of #1 quality, long-fiber kapok, or of a mixture of cork and rubber, hand or machine wound with a fine quality twisted yarn and covered with latex or rubber cement. Or the center of the ball may be made of other materials approved by the IJRC on softball. The cover of the ball must be the finest quality, #1 chrome-tanned horsehide or cowhide, cemented to the ball by application of cement to the underside of the cover and sewed with waxed thread of cotton or linen. The ball's cover also may be made of synthetic materials.

9

FIELD

Dimensions

The softball field (Figure 1) is similar in shape to a baseball field, but its dimensions are different. The pitcher's plate is 46 feet (men) or 40 feet (women) away from home plate, and the distance between bases is 60 feet.

Plates and Bases

Home plate must be made of rubber or other suitable material in a five-sided figure 17 inches wide across the edge facing the pitcher (see Figure 1). The sides shall be parallel to the inside lines of the batter's box and shall be 8½ inches long. The side of the point facing the catcher shall be 12 inches long.

The pitcher's plate, made of wood or rubber, is 24 inches long and 6 inches wide. The top of the plate must be level with the ground. The front line of the plate must be the following distance from the outside corner of home plate: Male Fast-pitch—46 feet; Male Slow-pitch—46 feet; Female Slow-pitch—46 feet; Female Fast-pitch—40 feet.

The bases, other than home plate, are 15 inches square, no more than 5 inches in thickness, and made of canvas or other suitable material. The bases should be securely fastened in position.

GLOVES, MITTS, AND MASKS

Gloves may be worn by any player, but mitts may be used only by the catcher and first baseman. The top lacing, webbing, or other device between the thumb and body of a glove or mitt worn by the first baseman or other fielder cannot be more than four inches in length. The pitcher's glove must be one color and cannot be white or grey, but multicolor gloves are acceptable for all other players. However, gloves with white or grey circles on the outside, giving the appearance of a ball, are illegal for all players.

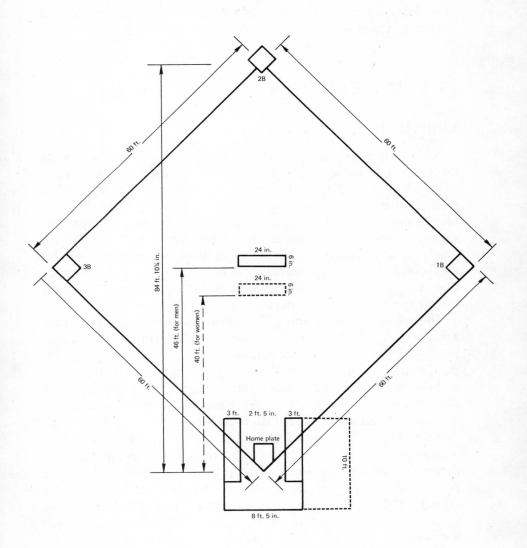

Figure 1. Softball field.

Masks MUST be worn by catchers in fast-pitch. It is recommended that catchers wear a mask in slow-pitch. Female catchers *must* wear a body protector in fast-pitch. It is recommended that female catchers wear a body protector in slow-pitch.

PLAYING CLOTHES

Uniforms

According to ASA regulations, all players on a team will wear uniforms that are identical in color, trim, and style. Ball caps are required for male players, and any part of an undershirt exposed to view shall be of a uniform solid color. If worn by more than one player, undershirts must be identical in color. No player shall wear ragged, frayed, or slit sleeves on exposed undershirts or uniform shirts. Also, catchers must wear caps; helmets are permissible for catchers, batters, and base runners. For safety and injury prevention, exposed jewelry, such as wrist watches, bracelets, and neck chains must not be worn during a game.

Though softball uniforms are as varied as tastes and styles, there are a few important points to remember. Uniforms serve two purposes—to provide some protection to the athlete and to provide maximum comfort. No article of the uniform should be restrictive or binding. If anything is too tight, discard it for a larger, looser item; if anything is binding, do the same. Size is of the utmost importance. Think of comfort rather than fit; if the trousers flatter, that's fine; but if they bind to flatter, that's not fine at all.

Joan adds that many pitchers wear long-sleeved sweat shirts underneath their uniform shirts to keep their arms warm. This is especially important on chilly nights when the perspiration may evaporate quickly, leaving a sore or "bound" arm. Muscles must be loose and warm to function properly, and, if the uniform shirt will not accomplish this by itself, it is wise to wear an undergarment.

Players with a history of pulled muscles, especially in the legs and thighs, may want to add precautionary taping with an elastic ban-

Joan at the end of a pitch. She is dressed in a regulation uniform.

John at bat in regulation uniform.

14

dage to their pregame preparation. Taping will give their vulnerable area additional support and protection.

Shoes

Shoes may be made with uppers of canvas or leather or similar materials. The soles may be smooth or studded with soft- or hard-rubber cleats. Ordinary metal sole and heel plates may be used if the spikes on the plates do not extend more than 3/4 inch from the sole or heel of the shoe. Shoes with rounded metal spikes are illegal.

Spikes or cleats are necessary, but the style of shoe is left to the athlete. Some prefer longer spikes, others short, nubby cleats. The condition of the playing surface—dry, damp, artificial, etc.—should determine the type of shoe that is worn.

Thick, high stockings are recommended to prevent accidental spike wounds about the ankles, as well as for protection against callouses on the soles of the feet. And fungicide-type foot powder should be applied both before and after a game to prevent the infection known as athlete's foot.

chapter three

A pitched softball is not easy to hit. It is delivered fast, and the pitcher is so close to the plate, the ball arrives nearly before the batter has a chance to think what's happening. The pitcher, of course, doesn't do anything to make hitting the softball any easier (except in slow-pitch softball, which will be discussed in a later chapter).

THE DELIVERY

There are three basic variations on the delivery of a pitch in regulation softball—the slingshot, the windmill and the figure-eight. Of these, the slingshot is designed to emphasize control. The

pitching

windmill and the figure-eight are, perhaps, more showy and spectacular, and they probably generate more speed but they do not lend
themselves to maximum control.

Of course, most top pitchers have developed their own variations
on the fundamental styles through years of practice. And no two
pitchers throw exactly the same, no matter which delivery they
choose to adopt.

Types of Delivery

THE SLINGSHOT. In the slingshot, the arm, gripping the ball,
leaves its position at the waist and is brought directly backwards to
the stretching point; then, it is moved forward with as much speed

The slingshot delivery. To appreciate the amount of ground covered by the pitcher, note the position of the bat in the background.

and force as possible. It is at this most-forward position, with as much drive as can be produced, that the ball is released. The arm does not define a full circle before the ball is released; the thrust—as the term, slingshot, implies—is confined to a short, powerful stroke that takes place below the level of the shoulder.

This gives the pitcher increased control over his or her pitch. When the ball hand describes a full circle in the pitch, the arm deviates from the "groove" that affords maximum control. But, in the slingshot delivery, the body does not have a chance to waver out of that groove, because the arm is not going to be pulling the body off balance.

18

THE WINDMILL. The windmill begins, as do all softball deliveries, with the ball hand resting at the pitcher's waist; indeed, both hands are together at the waist, loosely gripping the ball. Then the pitching hand is brought up over the head, as high as the arm can reach and all the way back—to describe a large circle. This allows a buildup of momentum before the ball is released that increases the force and speed of the pitch. But, because the arm has been moving so quickly, with such force, and in so large an area, the accuracy of each pitch is far less predictable than in the slingshot delivery.

THE FIGURE-EIGHT. The figure-eight is a combination, so to speak, of both slingshot and windmill deliveries. Again, the starting position is with both hands held loosely together, gripping the ball, at the belt buckle.

At the onset of delivery, the ball hand moves backwards quickly, as in the slingshot. But, unlike the slingshot, it does not come directly forward again. Rather, it describes a figure-eight pattern: The arm swings out and away from the body, so that it approaches the body again at an angle, usually a full-stretch distance opposite the hip. Then, as the pitch is to be released, the arm swings in again close to the body and directly at the batter.

This, too, increases the speed with which the ball hurtles toward the batter; but, because of the somewhat contrived motion of delivery, control often suffers. The figure-eight, unless it fits your style naturally, is perhaps the most difficult of the three basic deliveries to control and should be attempted only after careful consideration and extended practice.

It is recommended that the beginning pitcher undertake figure-eight and windmill deliveries only after the slingshot has been mastered. By then, however, neither the figure-eight nor the windmill will be necessary, since a pitcher almost never employs more than one style of delivery.

Delivery Style

In regulation fast-pitch softball, most accomplished pitchers master between four and seven different pitches. However, the

Joan Joyce's stance just before she delivers a pitch. At right a close-up of her feet.

21

(Above and facing page). A pitch from windup to follow-through.

delivery of each pitch involves the same motion, and, in almost all cases, the ball is held the same way, as well. Indeed, top pitchers do not tip off any pitch by their stance, grip, motion, release, or follow-through. "If I'm throwing a rise-ball, it looks just the same as when I'm throwing a 'drop'," says Joan, "and, by the time they know which it is, it's past them."

Joan's uniform style and delivery were proven in a study by a friend working on a doctoral thesis at the University of California. "She was doing all kinds of studies on pitchers in softball," Joan recalls, "the footwork, how far the arm goes back, how the ball is held, everything. She said I was the only one who was so consistent in stepping out to exactly the same spot every single time. At no time was there ever a giveaway. Even the velocity is the same for every pitch, except, of course, for a change-up (change-of-pace pitch) or a knuckle ball."

The ball is also held the same for different pitches, or, if there is

any change at all, it is far from radical. Joan uses the traditional two-finger grip for all her pitches—thumb on top of the ball and index and middle fingers gripping it underneath. Applying different spin or rotation to the ball at the point of its release is what causes the different action of the several pitches, and the spin is achieved with the motion of the arm and wrist rather than with the fingers.

This spin of the ball through the air causes it to do different things. The ball must "grab the air" in a certain way to achieve the desired pitch, an effect produced mostly by the seams of the ball. Depending on how the seams catch the air, the ball curves or rises or drops. The only exception to this rule is the knuckle ball, which is gripped differently but released the same way.

KINDS OF PITCHES

The best pitch is one that travels through more than one "plane" en route to the batter, ideally, dipping or rising to a different plane just before it reaches home plate. The fast-pitch softball pitcher's repertoire will include the following assortment of pitches: The drop, the rise, the curve (almost never used by itself), and the knuckle ball (used primarily as a change-of-pace). A straight fast ball, one which comes in with "nothing on it" (no spin), is almost never used. The softball is large enough that even the shorter distance between the pitcher's mound and home plate cannot adequately compensate for the pitch that comes in straight and flat.

The Drop-pitch

This is somewhat similar to the "sinker" pitch used by many baseball pitchers, but it drops much more abruptly and noticeably. As Joan said earlier, this is the favorite pitch of many top stars, for when thrown properly and with maximum velocity, it is almost impossible to hit.

Imagine yourself at bat, when the following happens: The ball, released by the pitcher, comes at you hard and fast but apparently on a line. You time the ball, locating its arrival point at ap-

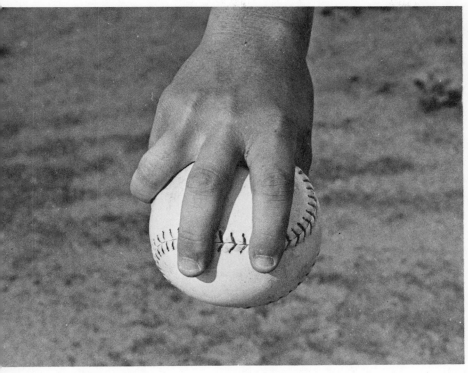

Proper grip on ball to throw a drop-pitch.

proximately shoulder height. Then you swing, but the ball has suddenly dropped to the level of your waist, a drop of a foot or more. Needless to say, you miss.

This, then, is the drop-ball, and here's how to throw it: "I do nothing at all to throw a drop," says Joan. "Using my two-finger grip, I just let the ball roll off the fingers. Oh, I may pull my hand up at the last second, just to get the ball to spin a bit more, but usually just releasing it with that underhand motion will get enough rotation on it. When I follow through, my hand will come up in a direct line. If I continued the motion, to exaggerate it so that someone could see the mechanics, my arm would go right over my head. That's the drop-pitch; there's almost nothing to do but let it go."

25

Proper grip on ball to throw a rise-pitch.

The Rise-pitch

The rise is, for all intents and purposes, the opposite of the drop. It might approach you at waist height, but suddenly "take off" and cross the plate on a line with your shoulder or chin. When it is coupled with a curve ("I use the rise-curve a lot," Joan says), it is also nearly impossible to hit consistently.

"The rise, or sometimes rise-curve, is still thrown with my two-finger style," Joan explains. "The index finger is the key to this pitch. I place it somewhat 'up' on the ball, almost as though I'm holding the side of the ball rather than the bottom of it. As I release the pitch, I force my index finger up and to the left, to get the ball spinning in a counterclockwise direction."

26

The Curveball

Until 1972, the mound was 38 feet from home plate in women's major league softball. (Men pitched from 46 feet away, then and now.) When it was moved back 2 feet, many more pitchers developed many more wicked curve balls.

The curve ball and the rise are thrown almost identically, and, frequently, the two are combined. One of Joan's most feared pitches is her rise-curve. "At a distance of 38 feet, my curve just didn't break in time," Joan explains. "It just wouldn't really curve well until it got past the batter, which, of course, was too late. But, when we moved back two feet, the curve became an important and effective weapon. Now it starts to bend, to break, just as it reaches the hitter."

There are isolated instances when Joan will throw a normal curve, just to show the batter another pitch. Almost always, a regular curve will be a "waste" pitch, one that intentionally misses the strike zone but might cause an overanxious or insecure batter to swing, providing a bonus strike. "A straight curve isn't really a good pitch," she says, "because, while it does curve, it does so on the same plane. And what's the difference if the batter hits the ball with the middle of the bat or up near the end? Either way, the ball will get hit. But a regular curve now and then can catch hitters off guard, because they get conditioned to the ball either rising or dropping. Then, when one comes in without doing either, they sometimes aren't ready and cannot adjust."

The rise-curve is thrown with both the index and middle fingers gripping the "side" of the ball and is released with a brisk snap of the wrist. The additional spin forces the ball not only to rise but to break, or curve, as well. "I have gone from using the curve as a waste pitch to making the rise-curve my most-used pitch," Joan adds. "I'd say I throw the rise-curve more than any other pitch now."

Joan has one word of caution: "When first throwing the curve, be careful not to 'break it off' too abruptly. It puts a great strain on the part of your arm from the elbow to the shoulder, and, especially if you're not accustomed to it, you can wind up with a sore arm."

Proper grip for throwing a knuckle ball.

The Knuckle Ball

The ball is gripped totally differently to throw a "knuckler." The pitcher grips the ball with the thumb and the small finger on either "side," so to speak. The middle three fingers, bent toward the palm, cradle the ball on the first knuckle joints. At release, the middle three fingers are kept still while the thumb and small finger simply let the ball go. As a result, the knuckle ball "floats" up to the batter far more slowly than any other pitch, and, because it has, relatively, no spin, it performs according to the vagaries of the atmospheric conditions (i.e., wind, heaviness or lightness of air). While unpredictable ("No knuckler ever behaves the same way twice," Joan says), it is most difficult to follow, much less hit.

It might be added, however, that there is a corresponding problem for the catcher; handling the knuckler is extremely difficult. Consequently, it is seldom used with runners on base or in critical moments late in a close game. Not only is it difficult to catch, but its slow approach to the batter is an invaluable aid to those attempting to steal a base. The catcher's time to throw to the next base and cut down a would-be steal is, obviously, greatly reduced if he must first wait for the arrival of a slow-moving knuckle ball.

Another method of throwing the knuckle ball, and one which Joan has come to use more frequently, does not involve the knuckles. Therefore, though the ball behaves like a knuckle ball, it isn't really one. "What I'll do is hold the ball loosely with the tips of all my fingers," she explains. "Then I'll sort of regrip with my thumb, allowing the ball to rest on the tips of the other four fingers, and I'll release it that way, with no spin at all—but with no knuckle push at all, either. It acts just like a knuckler, maybe even more unpredictably. I've seen a good one go right past the batter and the catcher without being touched. Obviously, I'd never use it in pressure situations, especially with a runner on third. But it's really difficult to hit, and I enjoy using it as a change-of-pace pitch."

The Importance of Different Pitches

Most top-level softball pitchers agree that a wide arsenal of pitches is not absolutely necessary. Softball pitches seldom act the same way twice in succession. Sometimes the knuckle ball will move a lot; other times it will have just minimal "action." Sometimes the in-shoot will break at an acute angle; other times it will just "roll" down, or in, in a lazy arc. The rise may pick up quickly and zoom past a batter's eyes, or it may move up just slightly, deviating a fraction from its straight plane of delivery.

Much of the variation is a result of the atmosphere on a particular day or night. Heavy air, humid and close, will adversely affect a pitch designed to move, will, in effect, slow it down both in velocity and movement. On the other hand, light air will act as a

Joan is shown here in the intermediate phases of a pitch. Although she says strength does not play a large role in pitching excellence, it is obvious that concentration does.

catalyst to such a pitch, increasing its speed and enhancing its movements and gyrations. But pitchers can take comfort in the fact that on hot, muggy nights a batted ball will not carry for as great a distance as on a "light," dry-air night.

Further, the top pitchers agree unanimously that size and strength have much less to do with success than is generally believed. They point, instead, to coordination—the ability to coordinate all body motions necessary in delivering a pitch—as the key factor. Joan believes that physical strength "plays some part in it, but I don't think a whole lot." She offers two examples to defend her theory: "Another girl on my team, another pitcher, throws exactly the same way I do. We both use the slingshot delivery, and we both throw the same kinds of pitches. But we're totally different pitchers, though not many people know that, or could tell.

"Somebody just coming out to watch a softball game, without being able to analyze what we're doing, would say we both throw the same way and that we're equally effective. The most they'd be able to see is that she uses her drop much more than I do. She has to rely on the drop, because she doesn't throw that good a rise-ball. I throw many more rise-balls. Other than that, we look like we're doing the same thing.

"But she throws with a lot of physical strength. She's a strong girl. I'm not, but I throw smooth. I don't use a lot of unnecessary effort in any of my pitches. If there's strength involved at all in a critical sense, it comes from my legs, pushing me off the mound and adding momentum to my body, and therefore to my pitch, as it is thrown.

"Secondly, look at Sandy Koufax, probably the greatest fast-ball pitcher in the history of major-league baseball. He wasn't physically imposing, yet he had a great, almost incredible fast ball. Much bigger men—heavier, taller, longer arms—had no fast ball even comparable to his. It's all in that quirk of coordination."

THE FOLLOW-THROUGH

A correct follow-through is essential. Not only must the pitcher

Joan in follow-through position. Though the force of the pitch has carried her to a position with both feet off the ground, when she comes down, she'll be ready for action. Note the position of her pitching arm, twisted to put spin on the ball.

maintain control of the pitch just released, but he or she must also be in proper position as a fielder, for as soon as a pitch is let fly, the pitcher is a fielder. Pitchers have won or lost their own games with prowess—or lack of it—afield.

There are a few guiding principles to remember in acquiring a proper follow-through. First of all, remain alert. Even a "waste pitch" might be reached by a clever batter, and, if you aren't expecting a ball to come zooming at your head, you could wind up a loser in more ways than one.

Secondly, you must achieve balance from the second of the release. Joan says her method is to come down with both feet on the ground—and facing the batter. Additionally, she maintains a stance on the balls of her feet, on her toes, if you will, with her eyes concentrating only on the batter and the ball.

Finally, it is essential that whatever delivery you choose, it is one that does not continually force you into an off-balance, awkward position as you release the ball. "This last point comes with practice," Joan explains. "As you release the ball, you'll find more and more that a groove has been established. If you are always in an awkward position, you must modify your delivery. A softball delivery is a rather natural one, far easier than an overhand baseball pitch, for instance. It won't take much fiddling with your style to bring you into the proper position."

It is also important that the glove hand be up, ready for a line drive or a hard ground ball. To achieve the proper follow-through stance and then find your glove hand dangling uselessly at your side is self-defeating. Joan describes her overall follow-through attitude as one of "intense concentration." She tries to "be ready to field or catch anything from the second I let the ball go. You must be ready to charge the plate for a bunt, to move either left or right for a ground ball, to leap for a line drive, or to get to first quickly for a throw, if the first baseman has had to charge a bunt . . . or get to home plate for a throw if the catcher has experienced some difficulty behind the plate. I try to make my follow-through one of total preparedness, and I think the two most important aspects to work on are facing the batter immediately and being on your toes, ready to move in any direction instantly.

34

"Don't allow your pitching motion to carry you too far to the left or right. If you throw each pitch exactly the same way and if you master a proper follow-through, then you'll get it right every time.

"Face the batter, get up on your toes, have your glove ready, and always protect your area."

WORKING WITH THE CATCHER

Even in a neighborhood pickup game, the pitcher's best friend and closest associate is the catcher. In addition to the obvious duty of catching the ball, this athlete can do many things to improve a pitcher's game, to enhance his chances of winning, and to help him control the tempo of a game. "The whole success of any pitcher," says Joan, "is the catcher. There are so many things the catcher can do to make me a better pitcher, I wouldn't even want to think about not having a good one behind the plate when I'm pitching."

It is the catcher, for instance, who signals for a particular kind of pitch, and the pitcher seldom questions or rejects—"shakes off"—a catcher's sign. "I had one catcher, Mickey Stratton (now in the ASA Hall of Fame), who was an absolute tiger. I was young, and once shook off her sign for a drop. She called time, ran out to the mound, and began screaming at me. 'Hey, what do you think you're doing?' she yelled. 'You throw the drop, because I called it.' So she walked back, and I threw the drop, and we got a strikeout.

"An experienced catcher is the secret to any pitcher's success. The catcher is behind each batter. She knows each batter. She knows what pitch the batter doesn't like and what pitch the batter can hit. She also knows what your 'stuff' is like that day, which pitch is working well for you, and that's something you may not even be aware of, working on the mound, because your head is so filled up with other thoughts."

Confidence in a Catcher

It is important for a pitcher to have confidence in the catcher. Any time a pitch is called for, the catcher has carefully thought out the reasons for calling it. To shake off a catcher, especially an experienced catcher, too often is asking for personality problems between the two of you. Remember, the catcher is in a better position to know which of your pitches is working that day and how much trouble or success each batter has had facing you during that particular game.

"We had a young pitcher who thought she knew everything there was to know about pitching," Joan says, "and we had a young catcher who felt likewise. Every time the pitcher didn't like a signal, she'd shake off the catcher. It got so involved that they'd have a hassle each time a new batter was up, and finally the manager had no choice but to use a different catcher each time the pitcher was scheduled to work. Things like that are self-defeating, bad for the team, and cannot be tolerated. An older catcher wouldn't have had that kind of problem, but that same situation might not have existed with an older catcher in the first place. Experience is invaluable, and no one should question a performer who has done well and achieved a reputation over many years."

The catcher also has an obligation to remove as much of the mental pressure as possible from the pitcher. In any game, the pitcher's main worry is making the ball break the way it is supposed to and making it get into the strike zone. That's plenty. If the pitcher also has to be concerned with how each batter did before, what each batter wants and doesn't want, and what each batter's weaknesses are, the job becomes infinitely more difficult.

Providing a Target

Mechanically, the catcher should be sure to provide a "target" for the pitcher by placing her glove at the precise spot where the ball should arrive. When the pitcher can concentrate on the catcher's glove, it is far simpler than having to guesstimate the spot of arrival. "I don't like the catcher to move around much, either, once I'm in my windup," Joan adds. "Any movement is a distraction, especially when it comes from the person who is going to catch the pitch. Nothing should disturb a pitcher's concentration. Good catchers

John flashes signals as a catcher does. Note how easily the number of fingers can be read, but John has extended his glove to shield them from the opposite team's third base coach or a runner on third.

realize this and are almost motionless from the time I start winding up until the ball is released."

Signs

In most organized leagues, the pitcher and catcher work out a series of signs that denote different pitches. Signs, or signals, are as varied as teams, but the most common involve a number of fingers flashed to the pitcher prior to the pitch, each one corresponding to a specific pitch. One finger may mean the drop; two may signify the rise; three could be the knuckle ball; four might stand for the in-shoot. Combinations of these finger signs are commonly used to prevent signs being stolen by an opponent on second base, who, like the pitcher, can see the signs being flashed.

Combinations usually involve two, three, four, or more fingers being flashed, each sign offering a different number of fingers. But a prearranged system affects their meaning: In the first inning, for instance, the second set of signals may be "live"; in the second inning, the first set counts; in the third inning, the fourth signal is the valid one. Which set will be valid can be decided at the end of each inning, to avoid a fixed pattern.

PROPER MENTAL APPROACH

The proper mental approach to pitching is also immensely important. You must *know* you'll get the batter out. You must have supreme confidence in your abilities as a pitcher. You must want to succeed and you must enter each game knowing you will.

Some examples here are intriguing.

"One of the finest woman pitchers I've ever seen," Joan says, "was a girl named Louise Mazzucca. I mean she was just unbelievable. She had a rise-ball that made mine look like it comes in straight. But she didn't have confidence. It seemed to me she was always impressed by the level of play she was in, as if she didn't really belong up this high.

38

Confidence in your own ability is important.

Joan at the conclusion of a successful pitch.

"I played against her in California one year, and she struck out the first nine batters, in order, and nobody even came close to hitting her pitches. She seemed impossible to hit. Then, in the fourth inning, she just changed. She started walking everybody, then she began worrying about her control and took something off the ball, and we hit her. In the end, she lost the game, and it was strictly her own doing.

"I never worry about the batter, except to make sure the ball goes where I know it will do the most good. When I'm going right, there's nobody who can hit me consistently. I feel like that every time I pitch and, sometimes, when my stuff is really humming, I get the feeling that the ball is traveling at 150 miles an hour and breaking 3 feet. It isn't, of course, but confidence can do that.

"There are times when I know not only that I'll get a particular batter out but that I'll get her out on three pitches. If she missed my rise and drop by a lot the last time up and if I throw them as well the next time, I'll figure three pitches; that's all. And it works out that way. If you have found the right groove, you shouldn't have to worry about control."

Joan's point is well taken. If you begin to fret on the mound, that insecurity and uncertainty will translate into pitches that are less than the best you can throw.

chapter four

According to John Anquillare, there are two mental conditions you must achieve before beginning to talk about the mechanics of hitting. "First, you need concentration," he says. "I mean total concentration. You don't see anything but the pitcher and the ball. You don't feel anything except the bat in your hands. You don't hear anything. Period. You have to shut out everything else and really get into the situation. It's you against the pitcher. Either he wins or you do. Each time you go to bat, it's like an isolated little war. I look at my hits as victories and I consider each time I don't get a hit as a defeat.

"The second thing you must do is learn to be aggressive. By that, I mean you can't wait for the pitch you want, because, in softball, the pitcher is much closer to you than he is in baseball and he throws

batting

the ball even faster. So, to be perfectly honest, it won't matter what type of pitch he throws; if you wait for it too long, you'll miss it. A good hitter is going to attack the ball. Especially in softball, if you're a defensive hitter (one who waits), you aren't going to hit the ball well."

AT THE PLATE

"I'm a little different from the normal softball player," John says. "The normal player is guessing at the plate. He's guessing rise-ball or he's guessing drop. But the way I figure, guessing just can't work in softball. I played organized baseball, too, and then I was a constant guess-hitter. If I didn't guess right, I just didn't hit.

43

Here John is using his hitting skills to hit an outside pitch. Note his foot placement with the front foot extended toward home plate, which turns his body slightly in that direction, until follow—through (bottom).

"But in softball, I changed my attitude. I decided that if I hit the ball out in front of the plate, it wouldn't have a chance to rise or to drop. At that point, it's just a fast ball, and even major league baseball players will tell you that a fast ball is the easiest to hit. So I don't allow myself to take the time to guess. I'm lunging for the ball, trying to catch it before it reaches home plate, because that's when it's going to start doing its act.

"That's why I feel that being aggressive is the most important part of becoming a good softball hitter. Don't give the ball a chance, because then you're giving the pitcher a chance, and they don't need any edge at all—as good as they are and as close as they are."

Hitting to the Closest Field

Under these circumstances, "hitting the ball where it's pitched" takes on special meaning. "You can't wait for your pitch if the pitcher is good," says John, "because, even if you get the one you want, it may be thrown so well that you can't hit it anyway. So you hit the ball to the closest field. But that had better be explained.

"If the ball is pitched outside (to the side of the plate opposite the side you're standing on), you've got to go to left field with it (assuming, of course, that you are a right-handed batter). If it's down the middle, you hit it back up the middle. And, if it's on the inside part of the plate, you're moving away, pulling away, moving your hips along with your shoulders to 'pull' the ball down the third-base line."

Power versus Control

But, by lunging for the ball, doesn't a batter lose power? "Probably," says John, "but remember this: If you meet the ball in softball, you'll hit for a decent average. And, when I say I lunge for the ball, I mean with my entire body under control. The old theory of softball batting was to stand right up close to the front line of the batter's box, but I don't do that, and many of the top hitters today don't do it either. You'll find a lot of them standing in the middle of

45

Demonstrating a good batting stance John keeps his elbows away from his body and keeps his chin tucked in.

the box, maybe even on the back line. What that does is give you more time to lunge with a controlled body action. I take a long step forward with my front foot, drop my shoulders to keep the bat on an even plane, and just try to make contact.''

In addition, power hitting is not that important in softball. "You'll find a lot more singles hitters in the top softball leagues than power hitters," John explains, "and there won't be nearly as many home runs hit as in major-league baseball. It's just tougher to hit a softball. Even top major-league players have found that out.''

LEARNING TO HIT

"If I was going to teach someone how to hit," John offers, "there are a few basic philosophies I'd follow, too. First, I wouldn't even try to teach anyone until I saw him hit, or try to hit, for a reasonable length of time. The stances people use are almost all different, and how can I say mine is best? People said Ted Williams and Stan Musial had difficult stances to master, but nobody would ever argue with their results.

"I wouldn't even try to make adjustments in someone's style of hitting unless I saw, after a long period, that he wasn't making contact with the ball. As long as he's hitting the ball, I'd leave his stance alone. I don't care if he's hitting off one foot or the other foot, or if he's stepping away from the pitch or swinging under it. As long as he makes contact, he has the most important factor in hitting working for him.

"But, if he's not hitting the ball, then there are adjustments to be made. I would recommend a straight up-and-down stance without much of a crouch and without twisting the upper half of the body around to face the pitcher. Softball players and managers call it an 'open stance,' which means you're half-facing the pitcher with all of your body.

"You must keep your elbows away from your body, even if it feels uncomfortable or awkward at first. If your elbows are in too close, you'll jam yourself. And, because your primary thought is to

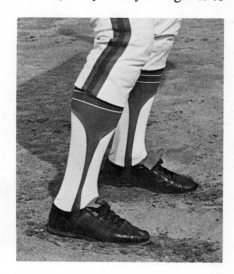

John's feet are spaced a natural distance apart for comfort. Feet should never be too far apart or too close together.

John's batting stance.

Joan's batting stance.

hit the ball out in front of the plate, to be aggressive, you can't allow your elbows to tie you up as you make that lunge-type swing at the ball."

Another cause of a hitting slump is moving the head. "It's something you probably won't even realize you're doing," John explains, "but, when you move your head, you're taking your eye off the ball. The easiest cure for this is always to keep your chin tucked in. When you're in the batting stance, your chin should be touching your shoulder, and, when you swing at the ball, you keep your head still. That way, your eyes will never leave the ball.

"One other thing, a basic thought. It relates back to baseball, too. Never swing up at the ball. You always swing down at it, because making contact in softball—we call it 'moving the ball'—is the most important part of a hitter's role. You'll make a lot more contact swinging down; you'll strike out a lot more if you swing up.

"After a while, if you start making contact, the power will follow. It's a case of getting into the right groove for you . . . of putting together all the separate steps of hitting into a rhythm that will work for you. And relax at the plate. You'll never hit the ball if you're nervous."

THINKING WITH THE PITCHER

While John doesn't consider himself a guess hitter, and intentionally strives not to fall into that category, there are a few methods he employs to anticipate what the pitcher will try to do.

In softball, the two primary pitches are the rise and the drop. John feels you can easily spot which pitch is coming toward you by watching the spin on the ball: "If you see the ball spin upward, it's going to be a rise-ball, and you should accentuate that downswing. But, if it's spinning downward (toward the ground), it's going to be a drop, and, while I wouldn't suggest that you swing up, you should try for a more level swing, to catch the ball within your even batting plane."

To do that, John recommends bending both legs. "That way, you get an even swing and you go down to meet the ball as it begins to drop," he says. "Add the fact that you should be out in front of the plate when you make contact and you can see the ball shouldn't have a chance to drop much before you hit it." In other words, instead of standing up straight and "scooping down" at the ball, you should stride into the ball with your entire body.

John also watches a pitcher closely. "After you see him a few times, you'll know what his best pitches are and you'll know whether he can throw a good off-speed (change-up) pitch. The important thing to remember is that a pitcher is subject to the same stress that affects a hitter. He'll worry when he's behind on the count and he'll worry if you've hit his best pitches earlier in the game.

"Also, in a crucial situation, as with men on base or if he's behind on the count, a pitcher will resort to his best pitch, his ace in the hole. An understanding of the game can teach you when the pitcher is in a tough spot, and an understanding of the particular pitcher

(Pages 51-53) John swings. Note that concentration is as important at the end of the swing as it is at the beginning.

52

will give you insight into which pitch he'll use when his back is up against the wall."

SIZE DOESN'T COUNT

There is no premium placed on size in major-level softball and with reason. "Your main asset, what you need most, is speed," says John. "When you do make contact with the ball, you must be able to run.

"When somebody hits a grounder to the infield, for instance, especially to the inside of the first or third baseman, it's a tough play for the fielders to make. If a guy has good wheels, he's going to beat it out for a hit. Since there is so much difficulty in getting home runs, you don't intentionally look for the big man, the strong man. In most cases, he's going to be slower than a small, light man. And speed counts here."

Joan makes speed count as she slides into base. (Courtesy ASA)

BUNTING

There is quite a bit of bunting in major-level softball. "Remember, the main responsibility of a hitter in this game is to move the ball," John states, "and, when you're facing one of the really tough pitchers, you don't often 'swing away,' because you just won't make contact with his pitches. So there is a great deal of bunting."

John's strategy in bunting is the result of several convictions. One, of course, is that to move the ball is better than not hitting it at all, since it places the burden of a perfect play on the infielders. Conviction number two is that most major-level softball players have great speed. Third, and perhaps most interesting, is that most softball pitchers have an inherent weakness: "They just can't throw the ball overhand very well," he says. "They never have to, and they get so used to the underhand, softball-pitch delivery that they can make lots of mistakes. You have to take advantage of everything."

Mechanics

The mechanics of the bunt are simple and basic. "You 'square away' your stance just as the pitch is released," John says, "which means you literally turn 45 degrees to face the pitcher. If you're a good bunter, the first thing you do is move your upper hand (the one away from the knob-end of the bat) halfway up the bat.

"In the beginning, you should simply try to make contact, but lightly. You don't want to hit the ball hard when you bunt; you don't even want to take a full swing, or punch at it hard. All you try to do is push the ball back toward the pitcher. Of course, as you become more familiar with the 'feel' of bunting, you'll find certain areas where your percentage is higher. Going right back at the pitcher is fine, but, if you can place the ball between the pitcher and the first baseman or between the pitcher and the third baseman, it's better. That way, neither man can make an easy play; he has to go for the ball. Your ideal bunt is when each waits for the other to get it. You can be on base by the time they realize it's hopeless."

55

There is a lot of bunting in softball.

John demonstrates the "squared-away" stance used in bunting.

To bunt, move your upper hand (the one farthest from the knob-end) halfway up the bat. Note that the fingers are in a "pinching" rather than a holding position.

Drag Bunting

There are other, more specialized kinds of bunting. The "drag bunt" is one of them, but it's only used by hitters who are batting from the right side, the first-base side, of the plate. When they try a drag bunt, they try to pull the ball along with them as they begin to run toward first base.

"What you want to do is to get a jump on the ball," says John, "in other words, to be able to start running as you bunt it, not bunt it first and then run. A drag bunt will be hit down the first-base line, and the closer to the line it rolls, the better it is for your successful hit.

"The catcher might have to come out to field it. Then he's got a tough throw, because he has to get the ball to the first baseman while trying not to hit you in the back with it. In softball, in almost every instance, the first baseman and the third baseman are constantly playing for the bunt—much more so than in major-league baseball. So, if you drag the ball down the first-base line, there's some confusion as to who should get it. There are great bunters in softball, because it's a high-percentage way to get on base. More important, it's the best way to 'move the ball,' and we are always trying to do that."

chapter five

The primary purpose for which every fielder exists is to handle a batted ball smoothly, cleanly, without error, and to make the play—whatever play is called for—that will turn a batter into an out. The bases in softball are closer than in baseball; hence the fielders have less time to throw out a runner going to first. Also, because the bases are closer to each other, first and third base are much closer to home plate. That would seem to make it more difficult, for example, to safely execute a bunt. But that advantage is negated by the fact that the batter has a shorter distance to run in order to reach base safely. To counteract the runner's advantage, the softball fielder must have quick reactions and thorough knowledge of the position he plays. When a ball comes to him not only must he *know* what to do with it, but also he must act quickly·

fielding

FIELDING BASICS

Throwing

Both infielders and outfielders should throw overhand. That spin gives the throw additional velocity, which sometimes will get a batter out by half a step. And an overhand ball stays straight; it won't curve or drop and it will be more accurate.

"It is important to plant your back foot and then come up straight before you throw," says John. "The second you may lose in straightening up will be compensated for by the speed with which the ball gets to the base. Throwing with any sort of a sidearm motion tends to make the ball either curve or drop, and both are diffi-

61

Both infielders and outfielders should throw overhand in most circumstances, and it is important to come up straight before you throw.

cult for the basemen to handle. Besides, they just don't get there as fast as the straight overhand throw."

Playing a Position

"I'd also like to mention this," John adds. "In any game, it seems, you have guys who can play several positions and do it all adequately, but this works against you if you want to excel at one. You have to be at one position for years to acquire all the instincts for it, to know the position well. No 'utility infielder' can ever become an outstanding second baseman or shortstop, because he doesn't have the time to master every minuscule detail."

When it comes to playing a particular postion, softball players play each position about the same as major-league baseball players do. "But there are very critical differences," John says. "There are different movements as far as coverage is concerned, although I have found that many major-league baseball teams—Oakland, for

example—have adopted the softball coverages as far as situational problems. In baseball, with men on first and second, previously, the third baseman held, the shortstop covered second, and the second baseman covered first. Now, in baseball, they're telling the shortstop to cover third, the second baseman to cover first, and the first and third basemen to charge the plate, playing for and anticipating the bunt. This is the way we've always done it in softball."

FIRST BASE

The first baseman, according to John, must have one thing going for him above all others—very quick reactions. In many, many instances, he is only playing 10 feet away from the hitter; he must play this close because most softball hitters will be attempting to bunt. So each time the ball is hit, it is a matter of reaction as to whether he makes the play or not.

The threat of the bunt depends on the count. "With no strikes on the batter, the first baseman must be as close as he can be," explains John. "With one strike, he takes a step or two back. With two strikes, he can move even farther back. The chances of a bunt are at issue here. With no strikes, chances are excellent. With one strike, they're still fairly high but not automatic. With two strikes, however, chances are minimal, because, as in baseball, a bunt with two strikes is an automatic strikeout if it goes foul. Only the very accomplished bunters will try it with two strikes, although, in certain situations, the batter might have to try it, even though it's dangerous."

The most difficult maneuver for the first baseman, though, is not fielding the bunt. "The toughest thing for him to do," says John, "is to get back to cover first when a shot is hit to third. Remember, he's always playing so close to the batter that, in fact, he's closer to home plate than he is to first. If a line drive or a hard ground ball is hit to third, the first baseman must make a complete pivot and run to first in time to take a throw for the putout.

"That's why the first baseman must have great reactions and

John Anquillare in the position a first baseman would take when anticipating a bunt—knees bent for quick action, hands low to scoop up the ball and eyes on batter and ball.

65

Quick reactions come in handy during a 1968 World Championship game, as a Mexican player tries for first. (Courtesy ASA)

speed. It's a hard thing to do, but what it boils down to is that he's responsible not only for covering the bunt but for getting all the way back to first, too. And having great reactions means he doesn't even need to think. The second a ball is hit—but not to him—he must get back to first base."

In fielding the area around first base itself, the most effective method is to crouch at the knees with both feet straddling the bag while waiting for the throw. That way, whether the throw comes in to his left or his right, the first baseman will be able to stretch in that direction and, in the same motion, position his other foot on the bag, so that contact is made and the force-out can be executed.

SECOND BASE

"In my opinion," says John, "second base is absolutely the toughest to play. The second baseman has to have very quick reactions and

In fielding the area around first base the best position for the first baseman is to straddle the base, one foot on each side, so he can react to either side and still keep one foot on the base.

John takes an off-center throw, but because he was straddling the base maintains contact with one foot.

he's got to know the position thoroughly, too. I've seen second base-men who are twice as fast as other second basemen fail to do the job. The reason? They don't have the reactions, which is something entirely different from speed.

"First of all, while he's playing back and not specifically covering the bunt, the second baseman must be aware of the bunt situation. If the ball is bunted, he covers first base—automatically. Therefore, he usually stations himself in the 'hole' between first and second base, but he will most likely 'cheat' one or two steps toward first base.

"Second, he comes up with many difficult situations. The toughest is when there is a man on first and no outs. Of course, it's a bunt situation, but while he's cheating toward first, what happens if there's a hard-hit ball? Let's assume it's hit to the shortstop. That makes it a double-play ball. So the second baseman must have

John in the second baseman's position comes up to tag second and then pitches to first to complete a double play.

quick enough reactions to reverse his direction, get to the bag in time to take the shortstop's toss, and then relay the ball to first base for the double play. This takes fantastic reactions, and I've seen some individuals with only half the speed of others make this play beautifully. It's all in the reactions."

The ball has beaten the Raybestos runner to second base in this play. (Courtesy Raybestos-Manhattan)

The shortstop must always be charging the ball, as John is doing here.

SHORTSTOP

"The shortstop, too, must have outstanding reactions," says John. "Compared to baseball, a softball shortstop can never wait on the ball. He has to be charging everything hit near him. Also, as in baseball, your shortstop is supposed to be the infielder with the most range. This can be defined as speed, I guess, or good reactions. But in any case, he has to be able to cover a great deal of ground to either side and also go backwards for many fly balls that don't carry deep enough for the outfielders to make a play. And he has to have a stronger throwing arm than, say, the second baseman, because there are going to be many times when he goes deep into the second-third hole (to his right) after ground balls. Then he has a long throw to first, and he must be able to rifle the ball quickly.

"The shortstop is the only softball infielder who has no responsibility on the bunt. He has nothing to do with the bunt except, of course, if there's a man on first, at which point he will either have to fill in at second or start a double play if the ball is hit too hard. And, if there are men on first and second, he covers third except, again, if the ball is hit to him.

"The hardest play for a shortstop to make is the high-hopping grounder between the pitcher and the third baseman. The shortstop has to charge those instantly, because, if he doesn't, the man is going to be safe. He has to get the ball while charging forward, then throw off-balance and across his body. It's a tough play.

"Generally, the shortstop plays between second and third. He may cheat one or two steps toward the second baseman, because the second baseman is usually cheating a step or two toward first base.

"Another of the shortstop's duties in softball, unlike in baseball, is to cover third base on a steal from second to third. The third baseman is almost always playing in too close, because of the bunt, and couldn't get back in time to take a throw from the catcher. In this instance, the shortstop must cheat toward third. With men on first and second, or just second, if a steal seems likely, he has to get a step or two head start toward third.

"One other point concerning shortstops: On the pop fly into the shallow outfield, he must suddenly play like an outfielder. He has to look at the ball fast, 'compute' where it's going, and then turn and run to that spot. It's much more dangerous to run backing up, because you not only lose speed that way but you can trip. So, in conclusion, it would appear as though the shortstop is the most versatile man in the infield. He has to play like a second baseman, a third baseman, a shortstop and an outfielder."

Here John flips the ball underhand to Joan as the shortstop would to start a double play.

THIRD BASE

Basically, the third baseman in softball has duties much like the first baseman's. And paramount to all of them is the bunt. "Again, you must have excellent reactions at third," says John. "No question about it; when that ball is hit, you don't have any more than a split second to react. When it's a left-handed batter and he gets into

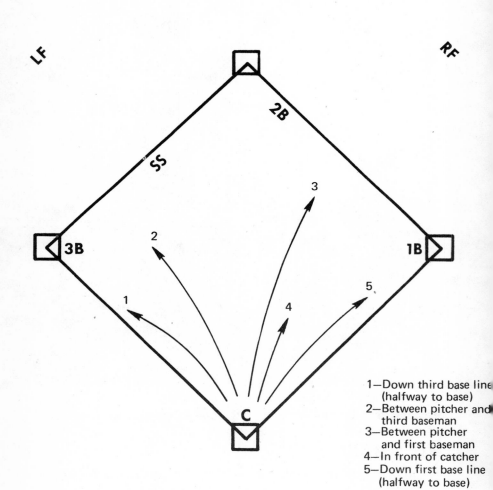

CF

LF

RF

2B

SS

3B

1B

3

2

1

4

5

C

1—Down third base line
    (halfway to base)
2—Between pitcher and
    third baseman
3—Between pitcher
    and first baseman
4—In front of catcher
5—Down first base line
    (halfway to base)

Figure 2. Likely placement of bunt.

74

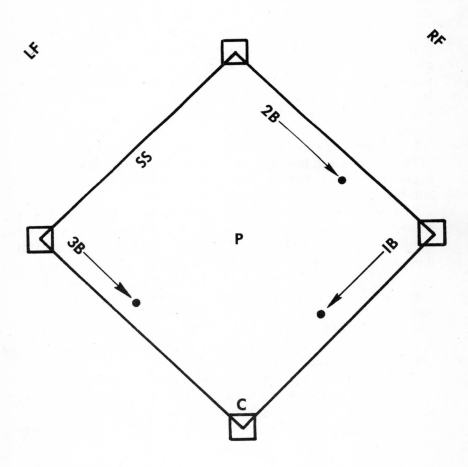

Figure 3. Changes in position of first, second and third basemen to meet bunt situation.

a pitch solidly, the line drive comes at you very fast and it's curving toward the foul line. If you've been playing for a bunt, you have to have outstanding reactions or you could get killed. The third baseman, like the first baseman, doesn't have to be extra fast. Remember, it's not speed that wins, it's reaction ability. He's got to charge the bunt and be able to throw off-balance.

"Also, the third baseman must have a great knack for anticipating the first baseman's moves. On a bunt out in front of the plate, for example, I've seen two relatively inexperienced men at these two positions actually bump into each other. They have to learn each other. Who's going to take the ball if it's bunted to the right? To the left? Ideally, the agreement should be this: The third baseman takes all bunts from the third-base line to maybe a little left of the pitcher's mound, because it's a heck of a lot easier for him to come across and throw in one motion than for the first baseman to get all the way out there, field the ball, then have to wheel around and throw to first. Split seconds count, always.

"There's an old joke about this position. If the third baseman's chest holds out, he'll have a good season. And, basically, there's a lot of truth in that. All he has to do on hard-hit balls is knock them down. It gets to him so fast, you see, that he can even fumble it twice and still have time to throw the batter out. So the most important move for a third baseman is always to be in front of the ball. Yes, use your chest if you have to. Just don't let the ball get past you, because then there's no one but the outfielders who can get to it, and by then maybe the batter is on second or third or a man has scored from second.

"His arm must be strong but not necessarily as strong as the shortstop's or as a baseball third baseman. The reason is that the third baseman so often plays in close, he cuts down the distance between the point where he fields the ball and first base. It's an easy throw, really."

OUTFIELD

John prefers to group outfielders in one section, rather than to segregate—technically—right field, center field and left field. "Outfielders don't necessarily have to have powerful throwing arms, but they must be very accurate," John says, "and the center fielder has to be the fastest of the three, because he doesn't have a foul line cutting down his territory. He has to go in either direction while it's not quite that much for a man in left or right. A left or right fielder can play off the foul line and just be responsible for balls hit between that line and the area where the center fielder will take over."

Positions

"The right fielder and the left fielder should play on a line behind the center fielder, and there's a very valid reason," says John. "The center fielder has responsibility for all the short-hit balls behind second base and the shortstop, so he's continually coming in. As a result, the right and left fielders must 'cover' for him, take over responsibility for the balls hit behind him into the 'gaps' in right-center and left-center. That way, the short gaps are covered by the center fielder, the long gaps by the right and left fielders.

"In softball, with the center fielder playing such a shallow position, there are more opportunities than in baseball for an outfielder to make a play at a base. He can throw a man out, but it demands an accurate throw. Any time the ball does get to the outfield, that man must act like an infielder. In baseball, often, you'll see an outfielder get down on one knee to block the ball and make sure it doesn't get through him. But in softball, he can never get to one knee. He has to charge the ball fast, field it on his feet, and throw it instantly. A man with any speed at all can make second base on a single if there is any hesitation or slowness on the part of the outfielder. He's got to make all his plays on the run."

Being Alert

"In softball, there's more of a premium put on taking an extra base by a hitter," says John. "In baseball, a man will hit a single, then take that nonchalant turn around first and stop; all the outfielder has to do is get the ball back to the infield, and he has time to make a rather leisurely throw, too. In most cases, the baseball outfielder

Even as the outfielder secures the ball, he's looking to see where to throw it and straightening to be in position to throw powerfully. By the time he is upright, the decision is made and he is already preparing to throw. The severe windup motion to the rear is necessary to insure a correct overhand throw; two fingers are positioned on top of the ball and a third near the side to steady its flight, once it is released. A good follow-through is also important.

Outfielder in position to field ball. His position is similar to an infielder's—knees bent, body low and both hands near the ground.

will throw to second on a single, just to keep the man from trying to advance. But he has time.

"In softball, batters are taught to keep looking for the extra base. So an outfielder must really charge a one-hop single, for instance, and come up throwing. And he must be able to throw quickly to second base, or the man is going to be in with an extra base and suddenly be in scoring position. In softball, with the pitchers so overpowering, one run is often enough to win a game.

In softball, batters are always looking for an extra base, so fielders have to be alert at all times, charge the ball, and come up throwing.

"Which means, of course, that an outfielder has to have knowledge. He's got to know where to throw the ball and when, instantly. He does that by concentrating at all times, by knowing what the situation is and where the runners are."

CATCHER

"Basically, the catcher's position is the same as in baseball, but

81

John demonstrates the catcher's squatting position with his glove hand in place to provide a "target" for the pitcher. Note that John's base hand is in a fist to avoid broken fingers from an unexpectedly fast or wild pitch.

there is one very critical exception," says John. "Baseball catchers more or less stay down in a squatting, 'rocking chair' stance. But, in softball, catchers have to be more versatile. With a good pitcher throwing 'live' rise-balls, the catcher will many times catch the ball over his head standing up; so he has to be more in a crouch than in a squat to be ready to spring to his feet when he sees what the pitch is going to do. And with a good drop pitcher, the catcher is constantly in the dirt, constantly blocking the ball. If a good drop-ball pitcher is on, that ball is going to be in the dirt 9 out of 10 times. So a good softball catcher has to be more agile than a baseball catcher and he has to have better reaction times, too.

"As for throwing out a runner, he doesn't have to have a strong arm, but it has to be extremely accurate. The accuracy is vital, because, if his throw to cut down a base-stealer is to the left or right, the man will get to base. There's just no play at all. The catcher has to be right on target, right down the middle, and catchers whose arms aren't consistent can hurt their team's defense dramatically.

"On bunts, that ball has to be almost dead for the catcher to come out and make the play, because he doesn't have the time to do it right if it goes any distance at all. But some might say he's the most important man on the field during any bunt, because he can see everything unfolding and the first or third baseman is just watching the ball. Therefore, it's up to the catcher to 'call the play,' to yell out whether the first baseman or the third baseman should get it, to yell which base he wants them throwing to, to act as the quarterback and play-caller. A silent catcher hurts his team, too. He's got the whole field in front of him; he has to tell them where to throw the ball. For instance, on a bunt with a man on first, if the ball is cleanly fielded, it might be able to cut down that lead runner. But the fielder can't see it, so the catcher has to make that decision. Then he's got to tell the fielder whether to throw it; it's his job."

IMPROVEMENT FOR THE RECREATIONAL PLAYER

Up until now, we have talked of a level of softball that most

John and Joan relax and practice by tossing the ball back and forth.

devotees don't play. But what of the athlete with a competitive drive, a desire to participate rather than resign himself to the role of spectator? How can he improve his game, utilizing hints and tips from the top-level players?

"Anybody can be a better player, whether he plays softball on weekends with his friends, for his company team, at picnics, anything," says John. "He can make himself a better player by thinking the game through. The most intriguing part of the game is trying to outthink the opposition, and you get a great feeling of satisfaction by making something work because you outsmarted the other side.

84

"Look for little things. Where is the third baseman? What pitches has the pitcher been throwing mostly? Does he use a particular pitch with men on base? When he's behind on the count? If you can establish some tendencies, you are ahead of the game, because not many players just out for the fun of it really think strategy. They're just trying to do their best.

"For instance, a particular batter, up three innings earlier, may have hit the ball to the right side. Now, if you're the shortstop, maybe you'll decide to cheat a little in that direction. If you do and he hits the ball right to you, it's to your advantage. You've turned his hit into an out, because you used your head. If you had stayed where you were, that ball would have gone through the infield and would have been at least a single."

chapter six

    Conditioning not only involves getting into and staying in shape, but taking proper care of your body in every situation.

STAYING IN SHAPE

To play any sport well, maintain a satisfactory physical condition year round. You cannot achieve top condition unless the same rules and practices become part of the daily routine. Yet this is not as dull and dreary as most people imagine. Conditioning does not mean solitary running over icy country roads or long hours in a gym lifting weights. And, perhaps surprisingly, most athletes have to watch

conditioning

their diet less than most sedentary people, because their daily activity level burns up a great deal of the calories others simply store.

Exercise

This is definitely true for Joan Joyce. "Other sports are what keep me going," she says. "I play a lot of volleyball, and I coach and play girls' basketball, and I find that if I simply keep active in these sports, as well as in activities like bowling and tennis, that I'll stay in condition. I don't do any specific exercises for my arms, because I have found you can more easily damage an arm than help it that way. But I find I do have to run a lot to keep my legs fit, especially now that they're 33-year-old legs."

John Anquillare also stresses running and suggests that for those without the proper facilities to run, running in place is nearly as effective. There is also a need for wind-sprinting; yet sprinting does not require a 100-yard track. "It's not the distance of your sprint; it's the effort you put into it," says John. "I feel you can get just as much benefit from wind-sprinting 15 or 20 yards as from doing a set of 100's. And almost anybody can find an area in which to do a 15-yard wind-sprint. Just do it over and over. It's the stop-and-go work that does you good, not great distances."

Other specific exercises recommended by John strengthen the shoulder, arm, and wrist muscles. This can be accomplished easily by squeezing a rubber ball over and over or by swinging a bat for a daily period of time. It's not difficult but it is important.

Diet

Diet, too, is something that seems to take care of itself—with some sensible precautions. "I stay on a high-protein, low-calorie diet," Joan says, "but it's not that rigid. If I feel like having a piece of cake or a dish of ice cream, I'll do it. But I use it as an occasional treat rather than daily indulgence. Dieting is just like bookkeeping. If you allow yourself to go into the red too often, you'll have a weight problem. But if you simply eat normally and are fairly selective in what you eat, the daily exercising and sports participation will take care of any problems."

LOOSENING UP

No athlete ever enters into a competitive situation "cold," without proper loosening up. To do so is to ask for pulled muscles, strains, or even worse injuries. The body is not geared to hurtle into all-out activity without some sort of preparation for this exertion. Muscles perform best when they have been warmed and loosened with gentle exercise, gradually increasing in tempo until all-out exertion is possible.

The length of time spent in loosening up depends on several factors, but, perhaps, the most critical one is the temperature. On

John demonstrates three of the stretching exercises he uses to loosen up.

warm days or nights, less loosening up is needed, but when the air is cool or a chill wind is blowing, considerable exercise is required to prepare the body for a competition.

For Pitchers

For pitchers, the most critical aspect of loosening up, or warming up, is the proper preparation of the pitching arm. "I have a regular routine," Joan explains, "and it changes only in the length of time I spend doing it. That, of course, depends on the temperature at the time. First I run, maybe back and forth in the outfield, maybe up and down along the sidelines. I don't run hard and I don't take long strides right away. You can pull a muscle if you stride too long or too hard at the onset. When I feel I'm warmed up a little, I stop running. But I don't stop exercising, because cooling off can be just as bad—or worse—than not warming up at all.

"When I stop running, I do some calisthenics, mostly stretching-type exercises. The one I like best is spreading my feet apart and then trying to touch my right foot with my left hand, my left foot with my right hand. That puts pressure on the long hamstring muscles behind the leg and thigh, and the hamstring is the one that must be loosened thoroughly. Some deep knee bends and maybe a bit of running in place will finish the calisthenics part of my warming up.

"Then I'll pitch, but never hard, never fast, and never at a rapid pace, until I'm completely ready. By then I'll feel a good perspiration, and, if we're not in the field first, I'll put on a jacket to keep myself warm until the bottom of the inning.

"I can usually warm up my pitching arm in just five minutes or so, but, if it takes longer, I'll spend as much time as I have to, because, if I tried to pitch competitively before I was physically ready, I'd be sure to hurt my arm. I can remember some cold nights when I just couldn't warm up even after the game started. I'd be all right for the first inning, but I'd feel like I was starting all over again in the second inning, and then in the third. On nights like that there isn't much you can do, but they don't happen too often."

92

For Other Players

Running is the best form of loosening up for all athletes, in general, since it puts into activity almost every muscle in the body. "You've not only got to protect your legs but condition and strengthen them," says John. "The guy who goes out before a game and warms up his arm, maybe, or takes some batting practice is very susceptible to leg muscle pulls or cramps. He's not loosening up properly. What I like to do when I first go out onto the field is run a couple of laps, then a few sprints. The first thing I always work on is my legs.

"The most important thing to do is stretch the leg muscles, the hamstrings and the quadriceps, because when they're stretched and warmed, it's not likely that you'll pull them. The most predominant leg injury in sports is a pulled hamstring, and I believe that a full 50 percent of them could have been prevented by a few simple stretching exercises before playing the game."

Finding Your Warm-up Pace

Warming up does not mean knocking yourself out. A tired athlete is just as prone to injury as a badly prepared one. Overdoing warm-up can exhaust an athlete prematurely, and only with experience will one learn the duration of time he needs. A sensible rule to follow is to stop running as soon as the slightest sign of fatigue is evident and not to overdo the calisthenics beforehand, either.

Joan also points out that the older an athlete is, the longer the loosening-up period should be. "I can't do today what I did when I was 20," she says, "and no one can. Your body can serve you well in athletics even into your 50s, but you must alter the way you take care of it. Most annoying injuries are the fault of the athlete, his negligence in properly preparing for stress. Younger players need less time to get ready; older players need more. It's an inescapable fact."

chapter seven

Until now, we have discussed only fast-pitch softball. But there is another popular form of the game, slow-pitch, which appeals to several millions seeking recreation without the prerequisite of superior athletic ability. Basically, soft-pitch and fast-pitch are played by the same rules. There are, however, a handful of major differences.

DIFFERENCES

The Pitch

The first and most significant difference is hinted at in the game's

slow~pitch softball

name—slow-pitch. In this form of softball, the pitch is required to be a soft, underhand delivery of the ball, which is meant to be hit by the batter. In fact, rules govern the pitcher's delivery: The ball must be delivered at a moderate speed underhand, below the hip, with a perceptible arch (from the time it leaves the pitcher's hand) of at least three feet before the ball reaches home plate; the pitched ball should not reach a height of more than 10 feet at its highest point above the ground; the speed of the pitch and height are left entirely to the judgment of the umpire.

There are penalties, such as the awarding of first base to the batter, if the umpire determines a pitch is delivered with excessive speed. Penalties may be as severe as removal of the pitcher for the duration of the game.

The Team

With the emphasis thus placed on hitting, official slow-pitch teams are composed of 10 players each, not 9. The additional fielder is called the short fielder, and, while he may be placed anywhere on the field, the most common station for this fielder is, as the name implies, somewhere behind or to either side of second base, in the "short," or shallow, outfield.

Other Differences

Other differences in the rules for slow-pitch softball include:

The size of the ball, which can be either 12 inches or 16 inches in circumference. In 16-inch slow-pitch softball, field dimensions are also different. For example, the base lines are 55 feet, not 60, between bases. In the case of women's 16-inch slow-pitch competition, the distance between bases-in-sequence is 50 feet. The pitcher's mound is 38 feet from home plate—for both men and women. In 16-inch slow-pitch, an arch to the pitched ball is not necessary, but the ball must still be delivered underhand at a slow speed.

Also, no base-stealing is permitted. Indeed, a base-runner may not even leave the base until the ball pitched has either reached or passed home plate, or has been hit. If he is found to be in violation of this rule (i.e., if he leaves base too soon), he is vulnerable to being called out.

THE PLAY

Since there are far fewer strikeouts in slow-pitch, there is a far greater emphasis placed on fielding, and because neither bunting nor base-stealing is permitted, the greatest burden is placed on the fielders.

"In fast-pitch," says John, "there are between 8 and 12 strikeouts in an average game. And, since we play seven-inning games, there are maybe one or two fielding chances for you during a game. Therefore, you're ready—though you really aren't, because it might

96

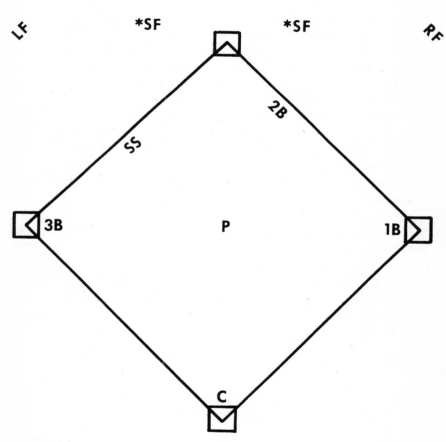

*Short fielder (SF) plays shallow outfield to either side of second base

Figure 4. Positions for fielders in slow-pitch softball.

be a strange field and you haven't had the chance for much infield practice, so you don't know how the ball will bounce and where the tough parts of the infield are.

"But in slow-pitch, you can get five, six, seven fielding chances—ground balls—during a regular game. Therefore, you get to be a much better infielder in slow-pitch because you have so many opportunities. The techniques for fielding the positions, of course, are basically the same. But the first and third basemen no longer have to play up close, because there is no bunting, so they don't have to be such spectacular fielders and they don't have to have those lightning-quick reflexes. With no bunting and no stealing, it takes a great deal of pressure off the defense.

"The third baseman plays even with the bag—sometimes even plays in back of the bag. The shortstop and the second baseman are relieved completely from those duties; can play normal positions and just worry about fielding ground balls and making the throw to first. And the first baseman plays his position just like the third baseman does, either even with the bag or behind it or over toward second, as in baseball, when a left-handed hitter is up."

The only strategy the pitcher uses is to make the batter hit the ball as it's coming down from the arc, which almost precludes the possibility of a long drive to the outfield. Or the pitcher may try to get him to hit the ball near the back of the batter's box, which keeps him off-balance and eliminates the chance to hit with power. "What he's trying to do," John says, "is to get the batter to hit grounders. That's all."

glossary

ALTERED BAT: A bat is considered altered when the physical structure of a legal bat has been changed. Examples of altering a bat are replacing the handle of a metal bat with a wooden handle or other type handle; inserting material inside the bat or adding a foreign substance such as paint to a bat. Replacing the grip with another legal grip is NOT considered altering the bat.

APPEAL PLAY: An appeal play is a play upon which an umpire cannot make a decision until requested by a player or coach. The appeal must be made before the next pitch, legal or illegal.

BASE ON BALLS: A base on balls is awarded to a batter by the umpire when four pitches are judged to be balls. The batter advances to first base without being able to be put out.

BASE PATH: A base path is an imaginary line three feet to either side of a direct line between the bases.

BASE RUNNER: A base runner is a player of the team at bat who has finished his turn at bat, reached first base, and has not yet been put out.

BATTED BALL: A batted ball is any ball that hits the bat or is hit by the bat and lands either in fair or foul territory. No intention to hit the ball is necessary.

BATTER'S BOX: The batter's box is the area to which the batter is restricted while in position to hit balls pitched by the opposing team's pitcher to help his own team to obtain runs. The lines that define the batter's box are considered inside it.

BATTER-BASE RUNNER: A batter-base runner is a player who has finished his turn at bat but has not yet been put out or touched first base.

BATTING ORDER: The batting order is the official listing of offensive players in the order in which members of that team must come to bat. The lineup card, on which the batting order is submitted, also includes the players' positions.

BLOCKED BALL: A blocked ball is a batted or thrown ball that is touched, stopped, or handled by a person not engaged in the game, or which touches any object which is not part of the official equipment or official playing area.

BEHIND ON THE COUNT: A slang expression indicating disadvantage in the duel between batter and pitcher. The batter is behind on the count when as many or more strikes than balls have been thrown, because he is more likely to be put out than to advance to first base. The pitcher is behind on the count in the opposite situation.

BUNT: A bunt is a legally tapped ball not swung at, but intentionally met with the bat and tapped slowly within the infield.

CATCH: A catch is a batted or thrown ball, legally stopped when the fielder catches it with his hands or glove. When the ball is merely held in the fielder's arms or prevented from dropping to the ground by some part of the fielder's body or clothing, the catch is not completed until the ball is in the grasp of the fielder's hands or glove. It is not a catch if a fielder immediately after he contacts the ball, collides with another player or wall or falls to the ground, and drops the ball as a result of the collision or falling to the ground. In establishing a valid catch, the fielder shall hold the ball long enough to prove he has complete control of the ball and that his release of the ball is voluntary and intentional. If a player drops the ball while in the act of throwing it, it is a valid catch.

CATCHER'S BOX: The catcher's box is that area within which the catcher must stand while and until the pitcher releases a pitched ball.

CHANGE-OF-PACE: An intentionally slower pitch, used on infrequent occasions, to disrupt a batter's timing. A change-of-pace which immediately follows a fast ball is apt to cause the batter to swing too early.

CHOPPED BALL (Slow-pitch only): A chopped hit ball is one at which the batter strikes downward with a chopping motion of the bat; if correctly executed, the ball should bounce very high.

COACH: A coach is a member of the team at bat who takes his place within the coach's lines on the field to direct the players of his team in running the bases. Two coaches are allowed.

DEAD BALL: The ball not in play is a dead ball. It is not considered in play again until the pitcher is within eight feet of the pitcher's plate and the plate umpire has called, "Play ball."

DEFENSIVE TEAM: The defensive team is the team in the field.

DISLODGED BASE: A base dislodged from its proper position.

DOUBLE PLAY: A double play is a play by the defense in which two offensive players are legally put out as a result of continuous action.

FAIR BALL: A fair ball is a batted ball that settles on fair territory between home and first base or home and third base; or is on or over fair territory, including any part of first and third base, when bounding to the outfield; or that touches first, second, or third bases; or that, while on or over fair territory, touches the person of any umpire or player, or that while over fair territory passes out of the playing field beyond the outfield fence. (Note: A fair fly shall be judged according to the relative position of the ball and the foul line, including the foul pole, and not as to whether the fielder is on fair or foul territory at the time he touches the ball.) It does not matter whether the ball first touches fair or foul territory as long as it does not touch anything foreign to the natural ground in foul territory and complies with all other aspects of a fair ball.

FAIR TERRITORY: Fair territory is that part of the playing field within and including the first- and third-base foul lines from home base to the bottom of the extreme playing field fence and perpendicularly upwards.

FIELDER: A fielder is any player of the team in the field.

FLY BALL: A fly ball is any ball batted into the air.

FORCE-OUT: A force-out is an out which can be made only

101

when a base runner loses the right to the base which he is occupying because the batter becomes a base runner, and before the batter or a succeeding base runner has been put out.

FOUL BALL: A foul ball is a batted ball that settles on foul territory between home and first base or between home and third base; or that bounds past first or third base on or over foul territory; or that first falls on foul territory beyond first or third base; or that while on or over foul territory, touches the person of an umpire or player or any object foreign to the natural ground. (Note: a foul fly shall be judged according to the relative position of the ball and the foul line, including the foul pole, and not as to whether the fielder is on foul or fair territory at the time he touches the ball.)

FOUL TIP: A foul tip is a batted ball which goes directly from the bat, not higher than the batter's head, to the catcher's hands and is legally caught by the catcher. (Note: It is not a foul tip unless caught, and any foul tip that is caught is a strike. In fast-pitch, the ball is in play; in slow-pitch, the ball is dead. It is not a catch if it is a rebound unless the ball first touched the catcher's hand or glove.)

HOME TEAM: The home team is the team on whose grounds the game is played, or, if the game is played on neutral grounds, the home team shall be designated by mutual agreement or by the flip of a coin.

ILLEGAL BAT: An illegal bat is one that does not meet official requirements. Examples of an illegal bat are one that has been altered or a baseball bat.

ILLEGALLY BATTED BALL: An illegally batted ball occurs when a pitched ball hits the bat at the time the batter has his entire foot touching the ground completely outside the lines of the batter's box or when any part of his foot is touching home plate.

ILLEGALLY CAUGHT BALL: An illegally caught ball occurs when a fielder catches a batted or thrown ball with his cap, mask, glove or any part of his uniform while it is detached from its proper place.

IN FLIGHT: Any batted, thrown, or pitched ball that has not yet touched the ground or some object other than a fielder is in flight.

IN JEOPARDY: In jeopardy is a term indicating that the ball is in play and an offensive player may be put out.

102

INFIELD: The infield is those areas of the field in fair territory that are normally covered by infielders.

INFIELD FLY: An infield fly is a fair fly ball (not including a line drive or an attempted bunt) that can be caught by an infielder with ordinary effort, when first and second or first, second, and third bases are occupied, before two are out. The pitcher, catcher, and any outfielder who positions himself in the infield on the play shall be considered infielders for the purpose of this rule. (Note: When it seems apparent that a batted ball will be an infield fly, the umpire shall immediately declare, "infield fly," for the benefit of the runners. If the ball is near the base lines, the umpire shall declare, "infield fly if fair." The ball is alive and runners may advance at the risk of the ball being caught, or retouch and advance after the ball is touched, the same as on any fly ball. If the hit becomes a foul ball, it is treated the same as any foul. If a declared infield fly is allowed to fall untouched to the ground, and bounces foul before passing first or third base, it is a foul ball. If a declared infield fly falls untouched to the ground outside the baseline, and bounces fair before passing first or third base, it is an infield fly.)

INNING: An inning is that portion of a game within which the teams alternate on offense and defense and in which there are three outs for each team.

IN-SHOOT: A curve ball that curves toward the batter.

INTERFERENCE: Interference is the act of a defensive player that hinders or prevents a batter from striking or hitting a pitched ball, or the act of an offensive player which impedes, hinders, or confuses a defensive player while attempting to execute a play.

LEGAL TOUCH: A legal touch occurs when a runner or batter-base runner who is not touching a base is touched by the ball while it is securely held in the fielder's hand. The ball is not considered as having been securely held if it is juggled or dropped by the fielder after having touched the runner unless the runner deliberately knocks the ball from the hand of the fielder. It is sufficient for the runner to be touched with the hand or glove in which the ball is held.

LEGALLY CAUGHT BALL: A legally caught ball is a batted or thrown ball caught and firmly held by a fielder with the hand or hands. A ball is not legally caught if it is caught in the fielder's hat, cap, mask, protectors, pocket, or other part of his uniform.

LINE DRIVE: A line drive is an aerial ball that is batted sharply and directly into the playing field.

OBSTRUCTION: Obstruction is an act of a fielder who, while not in possession of the ball or in the act of fielding a batted ball, impedes the progress of a base runner who is legally running bases.

OFFENSIVE TEAM: The offensive team is the team at bat.

OUTFIELD: The outfield is that portion of the field which is outside the diamond formed by the baselines, or the area not normally covered by an infielder and within the area defined by the foul lines beyond first and third bases and the boundaries of the grounds.

OUT-SHOOT: A curve ball that curves away from the batter.

OVERSLIDE: An overslide is the act of an offensive player when, as a base runner, he goes beyond a base he is attempting to reach. An overslide usually occurs when a base runner's momentum causes him to lose contact with the base; he is then in jeopardy. A batter-runner may overslide first base without being in jeopardy if he immediately returns to that base.

OVERTHROW: An overthrow is a play in which a ball is thrown from one fielder to another to retire a runner who has not reached or is off base and which goes into foul territory beyond the boundary lines of the playing field.

MOVE THE BALL: A slang expression for hitting the ball, making contact, even though the ball may be successfully fielded and converted into an out. Hitting the ball places the pressure of performance on the fielder, while striking out does nothing to jeopardize the defense.

PASSED BALL: A passed ball is a legally delivered ball that should have been held or controlled by the catcher with ordinary effort.

PIVOT FOOT: The pivot foot is that foot which the pitcher must keep in contact with the pitcher's plate until the ball is released.

PLAY BALL: This is the term used by the plate umpire to indicate that play shall begin or shall be resumed.

PICKUP GAME: A loosely organized game, not sponsored, condoned, or approved by any organized league, which involves the simple act of finding enough players to field two teams.

QUICK RETURN PITCH: The quick return pitch is one made by the pitcher in an obvious attempt to catch the batter off-balance. It is thrown before the batter takes his desired position in the batter's box or while he is still off-balance as a result of the previous pitch.

SACRIFICE FLY: A sacrifice fly is scored when, with less than two outs, the batter helps a runner score by hitting a fair fly that is caught.

SHAKE OFF: A slang term describing a pitcher's refusal to throw the type of pitch the catcher signals for. The pitcher will simply counter with a negative shake of the head, hence, "shaking off" the catcher, who will then offer another signal for another pitch.

SHUTOUT: A game in which one teams fails to score.

STEALING: Stealing is the act of a base runner attempting to advance during a pitch to the batter.

STRIKE ZONE: Fast-pitch—The strike zone is that space over any part of home plate which is between the batter's armpits and the top of his knees when the batter assumes his natural batting stance. Slow-pitch—The strike zone is that space over any part of home plate which is between the batter's highest shoulder and his knees when the batter assumes his natural batting stance.

TIME: Time is the term used by the umpire to order the suspension of play.

TRIPLE PLAY: A triple play is a continuous action play by the defense in which three offensive players are put out.

TURN AT BAT: A turn at bat begins when a player first enters the batter's box and continues until he is put out or becomes a base runner.

WASTE PITCH: A slang expression that refers to a pitch intentionally thrown outside the strike zone, delivered in an attempt to trick the batter into striking at a ball he will have great difficulty hitting.

WILD PITCH: (Fast-pitch only) A wild pitch is a legally delivered ball so high, so low, or so wide of the plate that the catcher cannot or does not stop and control it with ordinary effort.

index

U

Undershirts, 12
Uniforms, 12-15, *illus*. 13, 14
U.S. Women's Championship, 3

W

Warm-ups, 88-93
Waste pitch, 27, 105
Waterbury, Connecticut, x-xi

Weather, effect of on pitches,
    29-32
Wild pitch, 105
Williams, Ted, xi
Windmill delivery, 17, 20
Women's National Championship, xi
Women's softball, viii, xv-xvii, 10,
    12, 27. *See also* Competition,
    softball
Women's World Tournament, xii
World Championship, viii
    1968 team, *illus*. 2